3D PUZZLES TO CUT & CONSTRUCT AND SOLVE

ALAN ROBBINS

A Dell Trade Paperback

A DELL TRADE PAPERBACK
Published by
Dell Publishing
a division of
Bantam Doubleday Dell Publishing Group, Inc.
666 Fifth Avenue
New York, New York 10103

ISBN: 0-440-50143-1

Printed in the United States of America
Published simultaneously in Canada

December 1989

10   9   8   7   6   5   4   3   2   1
KPP

INTRODUCTION

The ten puzzles that can be constructed from the pages of this book are classics of a type of puzzle that achieved great popularity at the beginning of the century. The early 1900s were the heyday of sculptural puzzles produced in wood, metal, and paper. Many of them first appeared as advertising premiums or promotional giveaways. They became popular immediately, and the original versions have now become collector's items.

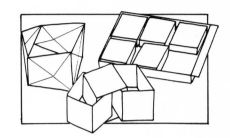

The beauty of these three-dimensional puzzles—and one of the reasons they were used so frequently for advertising—is their durability. They can be played with over and over again. In some cases, even finding the answer the first time won't help you solve the puzzle later on.

Now, with the publication of 3D PUZZLES, these classic mind-benders are available in an inexpensive new form. You may even find making them as much fun as solving them. Just follow the simple directions for construction and solution. You'll see why these puzzles started a craze back at the turn of the century, and why they remain just as popular today.

CONTENTS

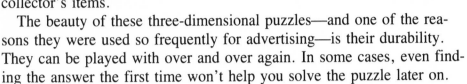

INSTRUCTIONS AND HINTS

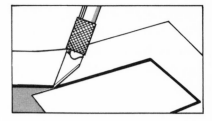

Each puzzle in this book is composed of a number of different pieces. These pieces are made by cutting out the patterns, called templates, then folding and gluing them into three-dimensional shapes. Cut out the templates, which appear on pages 15 to 43, along the thick black lines around the edge of each one using scissors, a single-edge razor, or a razor (X-Acto) knife. If you cut slightly to the inside of the line, so the thick line is cut off of the piece, your final model will look a bit neater and won't have heavy lines on it.

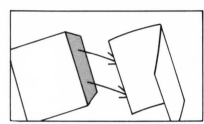

The thinner lines on each template indicate folds. *Don't* cut these thin lines; they are meant to be scored. (A score is a shallow indentation made along the line to make folding neater and easier.) To score along these thin lines, place a ruler on the line and press down the length of the line with the back of a razor or other dull edge. It will then be easy to fold along this crease. Be careful if you use the back of a razor. You may want to cover the sharp edge with some tape to make it safer to handle.

Each template also contains tabs that hold it together, or attach it to other pieces, in a three-dimensional shape. Simply spread a thin layer of glue on the tab to cover the complete tab area, then hold the entire tab in place until it is dry. Glue the tabs in alphabetical sequence when indicated. Whenever possible, the tabs should be glued to the inside edges so they will not show on the final model.

THE MAGIC PYRAMID

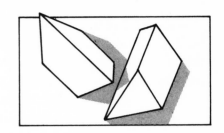

Let's start with one of the most interesting puzzles in the collection. It's a classic problem in solid geometry. A patent was issued for a version of the Magic Pyramid in 1940, but like most of the puzzles in this book, some variation of the basic idea had been around long before that.

The reason for its popularity is easy to understand. The puzzle's two disarmingly simple pieces create an intriguing challenge in spatial reasoning. It seems almost *too* simple. The solution is appealing, however, because the answer tends to come in a flash after a few moments of struggle.

MAKING THE PIECES

The two shapes that make up this puzzle are identical. Cut them out along the heavy outer line, then score all the thin lines using a ruler and the back edge of a razor or other dull edge. Crease along these scored lines and follow the diagrams at the right to fold the pieces into two identical wedge shapes. Glue tab A to the opposite edge to create a triangular tube (Figure 1), then bring the side flaps up and glue the remaining tabs to the inside of the model (Figure 2).

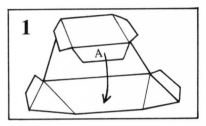

If you want the pieces of your model to be completely white, with no lines showing, fold them so the lines end up inside the model. Either way, you should end up with two identical triangular wedges (Figure 3).

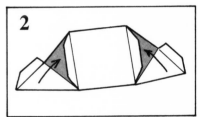

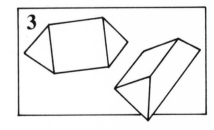

WORKING THE PUZZLE

All that's left now is the hard part . . . the solution. Just take the two pieces and try to put them together to form a pyramid.

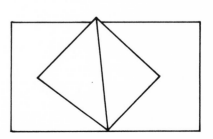

THE FOUR CUBES

This puzzle seems to come back into vogue with every new generation. Popular versions appeared in 1900 when the first patent was issued, during World War I showing the flags of the Allies, during the 1930s as an advertising premium for a food company, and again in the 1960s in a plastic version called Instant Insanity.

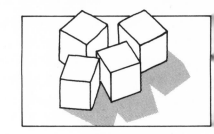

It's an easy puzzle to make in any material but, as you'll see, the solution is quite a bit more difficult.

MAKING THE PIECES

The puzzle consists simply of four cubes. These can be easily constructed using the outlines in the book. Just cut out the templates along the thick lines, then score and fold along all the thin lines. Glue tab *A* first to create a hollow box (Figure 1). Then bring up the sides of the cube and glue all tabs marked *B*, then *C* (Figure 2).

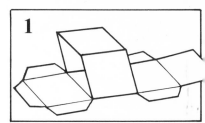

The extra square is glued last, flat down on the top of the cube to give it extra stability (Figure 3).

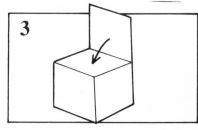

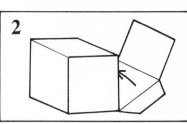

WORKING THE PUZZLE

Can you arrange the four cubes together in a row so that each of the four sides of the row shows four different symbols?

THE FLEXAGON

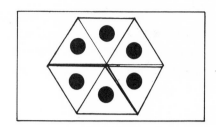

Folding puzzles of various kinds have been popular for decades. The relative cheapness of the paper on which they can be printed makes them ideal for mass production, hence their constant appeal as giveaways. Thousands of clever ones were distributed during World War II, for example, to promote defense bonds. Some people consider the simple road map to be the ultimate paper-folding problem.

The folding puzzle shown here is easy to make if you follow the directions carefully, but uniquely challenging to solve.

MAKING THE PIECES

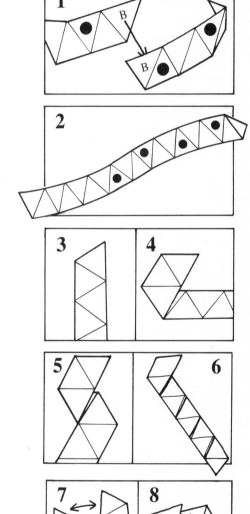

As always, cut the puzzle pieces out along the thick outer lines and score and fold the thin ones. Next, glue the three short strips into one long strip. Take the first piece and glue triangle *A* to the front, face to face, of triangle *A* on the second piece. Then glue triangle B to the back of triangle *B* on the third strip (Figure 1). When you're done, you'll have a strip with nineteen triangles on it, showing four dots on one side and two on the other (Figure 2).

Now follow Figures 3 to 6 at the right to fold the strip into a shorter strip, by twisting in the same direction along every other fold. When you're done, bend this shorter strip into a ring and glue the two end flaps together, one over the other, making sure that the two little arrows, one on the top side and one on the bottom, are pointing in the same direction (Figures 7 and 8). You should be able to fold your Flexagon completely flat. If you can't, redo the last step, making sure the two arrows are pointing the same way.

The folds in this puzzle take a lot of wear and tear, so if you want your model to last longer, put some tape over each fold.

WORKING THE PUZZLE

You should be able to fold, twist, and turn the Flexagon model in a dizzying variety of combinations. The challenge is to fold it so that the six triangles with the dots all face the same way in a hexagon, as shown in the top picture.

7

THE THREE RINGS

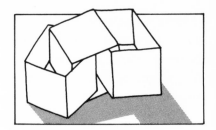

Here's a combination of two popular puzzle types. The logic it requires relates to the type of thinking used in sliding block puzzles. But the manipulation of the parts is similar to folding puzzles. The combination produces an interesting study in spatial reasoning.

MAKING THE PIECES

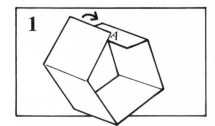

This one is extremely simple to construct. First cut out and score all three pieces. Then all you have to do is form strip *A* into an open cube with the dots on the outside, by gluing tab *A* to the underside of the opposite end of the strip (Figure 1).

Do the same with the other two strips, but before gluing them, loop each of them through the first strip as shown (Figure 2), to create a chain of three links.

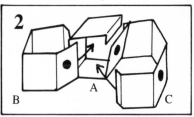

WORKING THE PUZZLE

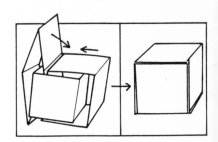

By folding, twisting, and tucking, it is possible to create a large number of cubes with this arrangement. But can you, without tearing or unlinking the rings, create a blank cube with no dots on it?

THE LINKED RINGS

Here's a simple puzzle with an elegant solution. It fits into the category called take-apart puzzles, which were extremely popular at the turn of the century. This type of puzzle ranged from simple wooden or fabric premiums bearing the sponsor's name, all the way to elaborate Japanese trick boxes.

The one reproduced here first appeared as an advertising giveaway for a cigar company back in 1892. It's easy to see why this type of puzzle was so common. The advertiser was able to keep the company name on view for weeks while the prospective customer struggled to find the answer.

MAKING THE PIECES

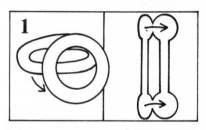

Cut out the four shapes of the puzzle (including the interior spaces), then fold each piece in half and neatly glue the two sides together (Figure 1). You will end up with one large ring, two small ones, and one dumbbell (Figure 2).

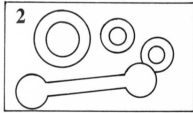

This puzzle is meant to be produced on heavy cardboard; that is the reason for doubling the weight of each piece. In fact, you can mount the dumbbell on a piece of cardboard to stiffen it even more.

WORKING THE PUZZLE

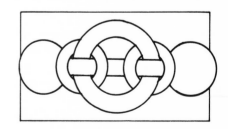

Without tearing or breaking any of the pieces, can you fit them together in the linked arrangement shown in the illustration at the right?

Another way to solve this puzzle is to cut a slit in the large ring, assemble the pieces in the linked arrangement shown, then glue or tape the slit closed. Now, without tearing or breaking the pieces, can you unlink them?

THE FOLDING STAR

Here's another folding puzzle with a tricky solution. A patent was apparently issued in 1943 for a puzzle of this kind, although similar varieties have appeared, as you might expect, before and since.

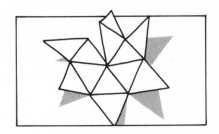

MAKING THE PIECES

This is one of the easiest puzzles in the book to make. Just cut out the star along the thick outer lines. Note that there is also a cut to the center from one of the edges.

Now score along all the thin lines and crease these folds back and forth for flexibility (Figure 1). These creases will be getting a work-out, so cover them with tape if you want the puzzle to last.

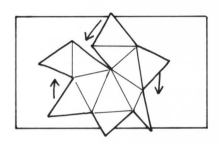

WORKING THE PUZZLE

All you have to do now is fold, turn, and flip along the creases until three triangles make a complete picture of the elephant.

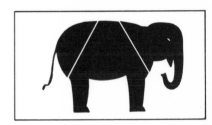

THE SLIDING BLOCKS

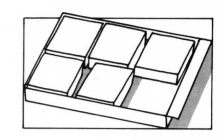

This is one of the most popular puzzle forms of all time. An early version, called the 14–15 Puzzle, by the puzzle expert Sam Loyd, became a major fad. A century later Erno Rubik's famous cube, a sophisticated three-dimensional variation on the same theme, returned the world to a frenzy of sliding blocks. In between, millions of sliding-block puzzles have been marketed in wood, plastic, and metal using every type of image and number sequence imaginable.

The sample offered here has the fewest blocks and therefore the smallest number of combinations. But don't get too comfortable; the solution still takes seventeen moves!

MAKING THE PIECES

There are six pieces in this puzzle, one tray and five blocks that fit in it. Cut them all out along the heavy outer lines. Note that there are heavy lines at every corner that must be cut as well. Next, score and crease along the thin lines.

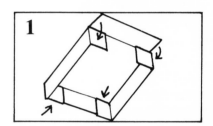

Form each of the five square pieces into blocks, by folding the sides down and gluing the tabs as shown (Figure 1). Then form the larger piece into a tray by folding the sides *up* and gluing the tabs at the corners. The extra flap on the tray is solid black and should stick out like a ledge (Figure 2).

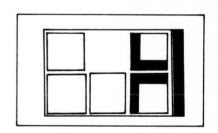

WORKING THE PUZZLE

Start with the pieces in the tray as shown at the right. Now, by sliding the blocks around in the tray, can you rearrange them to complete the black rectangular frame?

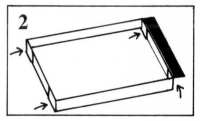

11

THE TESSERA

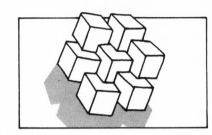

This is the most difficult puzzle in the book to solve, but it is also the most beautiful and worth a try.

It is based on a complex three-dimensional puzzle form known as the interlocking solid or burr puzzle. Thousands have been produced in complex geometric arrangements, usually in wood. They are related to the Japanese kumiki puzzles, which are sculptures made of complex interlocking parts, and also to the familiar plastic keychain puzzle.

MAKING THE PIECES

The puzzle is not difficult to construct, but it takes a bit more work than the others in the book. It is made up of seven solid cubes and four rings. First cut out and construct the solid cubes in the exact same way you did for the Four Cubes puzzle (Figure 1). Then construct the four rings by cutting, scoring and folding, and then gluing the tabs (Figure 2).

Next, follow the illustrations at the right to combine these into four puzzle pieces. Glue the space marked A on the first cube directly to the space marked A on the ring. Make sure that the entire gray area is covered with glue, and hold it in place until it is secure (Figures 3–4). Continue joining the pieces together in this way, then check with the illustrations (Figures 5–8) to make sure the four puzzle pieces are correct.

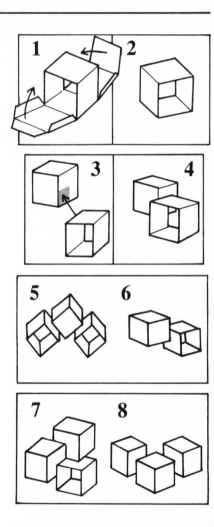

WORKING THE PUZZLE

Can you fit the pieces together to form the tessera shape shown in the illustration at the right?

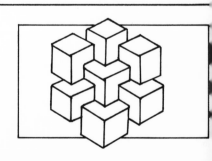

12

THE WALKING MAZE

Maze and route puzzles were another popular form at the turn of the century. They usually came in cardboard boxes and contained a "traveler," a small piece in metal or wood that fit over metal bumps or protrusions in the box and allowed you to follow the pathways. Pike's Peak Or Bust, an 1895 puzzle from Parker Brothers, is one well-known example.

Our version is paper, of course, but that won't make solving it any easier.

MAKING THE PIECES

Cut the large piece out of the book, then use a razor blade or razor knife to carefully cut around each of the small semicircles. Cut only on the curved line, not the straight one.

Next, score along each of the short thin lines at the base of the semicircles, then bend the semicircles up so they stand perpendicular to the flat surface (Figure 1). These are the bumps on which the traveler will fit.

Construct the traveler by cutting out the entire long strip. Remember to cut out and remove, carefully, the two circles at each end. Score, fold, and glue the handle of the traveler as shown (Figure 2).

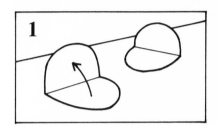

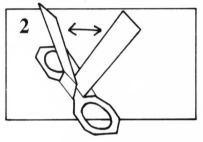

WORKING THE PUZZLE

Start by putting one circle of the traveler over the semicircular bump marked "start" and see if you can reach the end by twisting the traveler around only to any other bump it can reach.

Remember, one end of the traveler must always encircle one of the bumps.

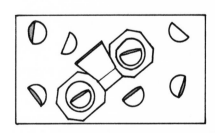

THE REVERSING CUBE

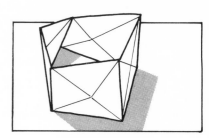

This one is a folding puzzle but, unlike the more common varieties, it involves some very complex three-dimensional reasoning. In fact, the twists and turns of this particular puzzle are so challenging that we'll even give you the answer first!

MAKING THE PIECES

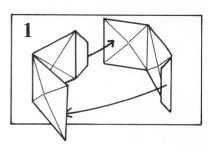

Cut out the two strips along the thick outer lines, then score and crease both ways along the thin lines. Glue the two tabs to their opposite sides as shown (Figure 1) to form the strips into a single ring.

This puzzle gets a lot of wear and tear on the folds, so you may want to strengthen them by putting tape on both sides of each fold.

WORKING THE PUZZLE

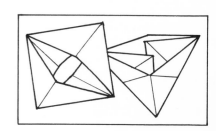

After you've played with the puzzle for a few minutes, you'll notice that it can be folded, squeezed, and turned in an infinite number of ways. The problem—to fold it in such a way that it can be turned completely inside out, without tearing or cutting it.

Sound tricky? It is. So here's a revised version of the problem, no less challenging. Look up the answer on page 47 and follow the steps of the solution. *Now* see if you can repeat the procedure and do it on your own!

THE MAGIC PYRAMID

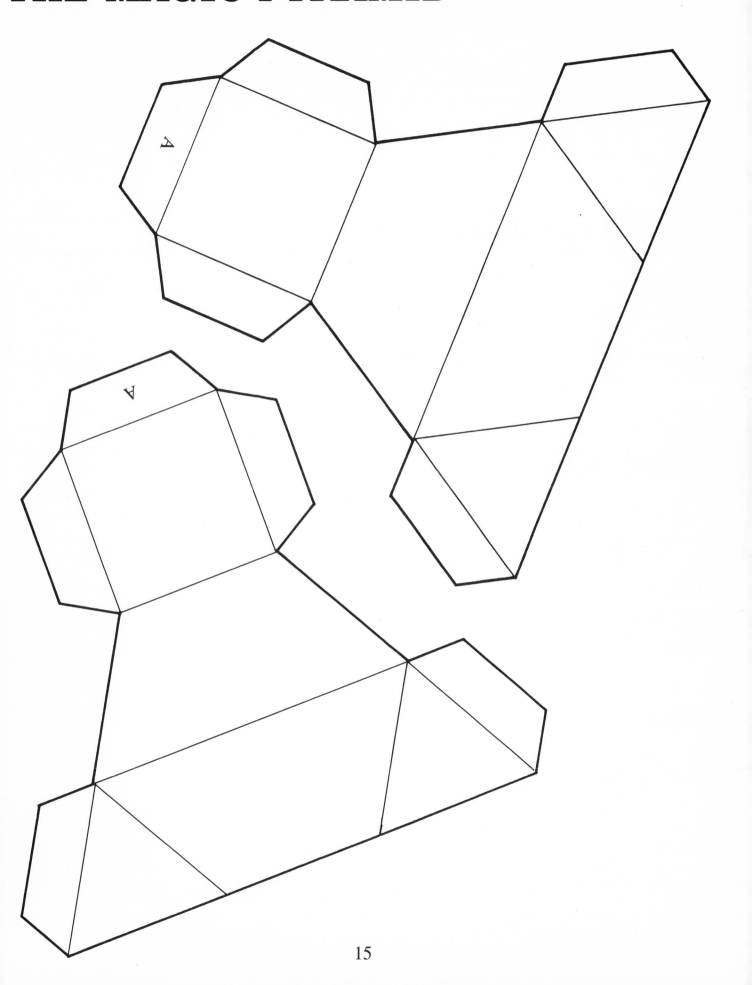

THE FOUR CUBES

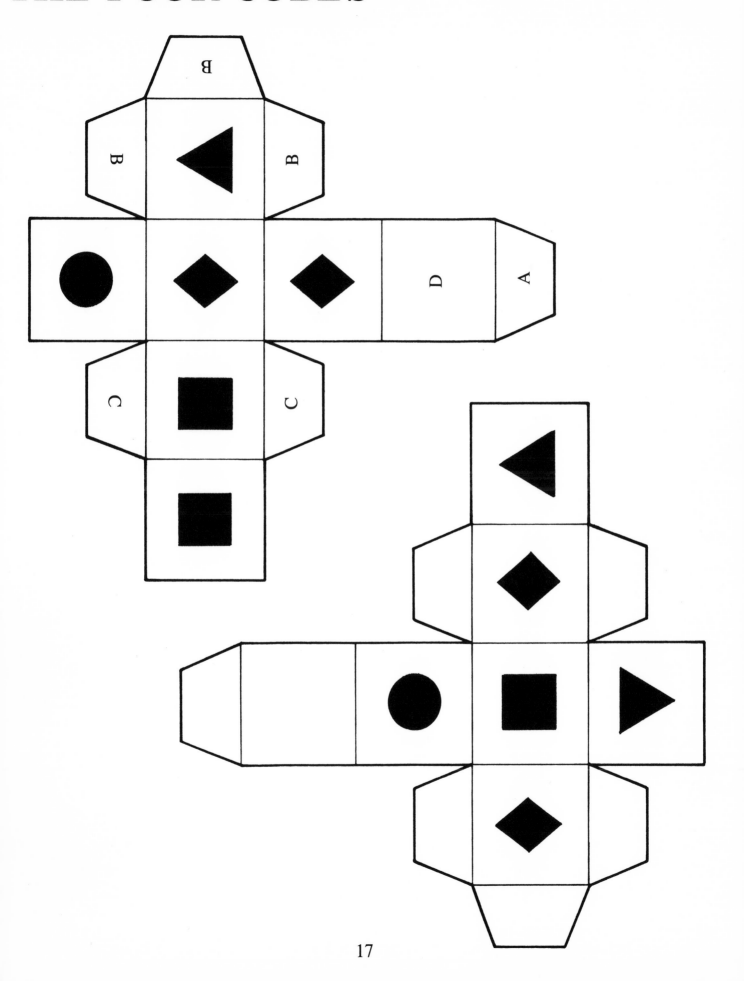

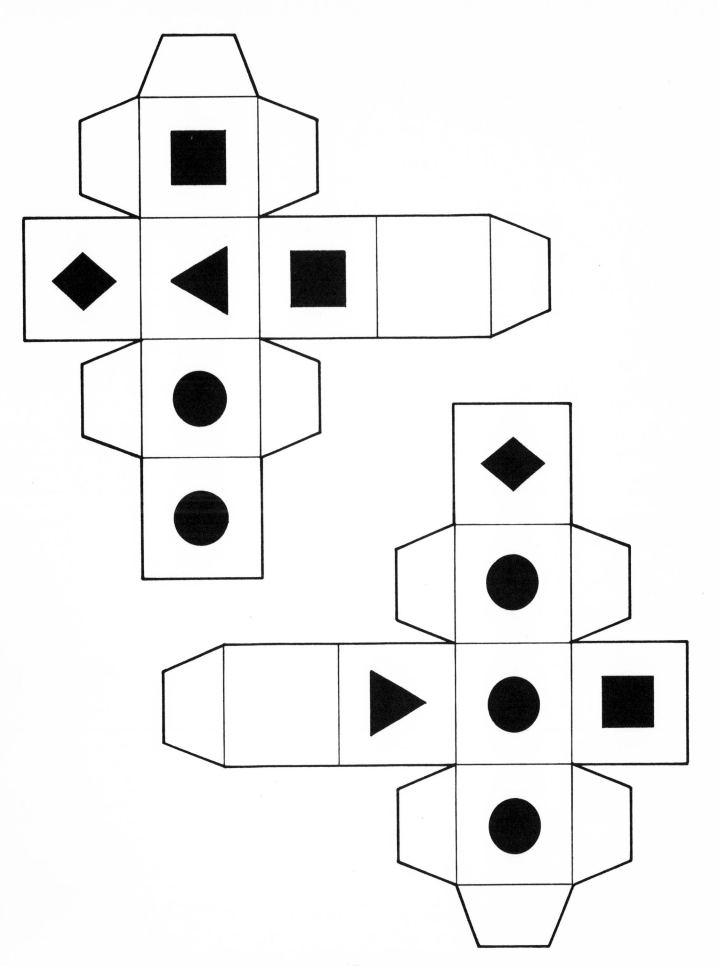

THE FLEXAGON

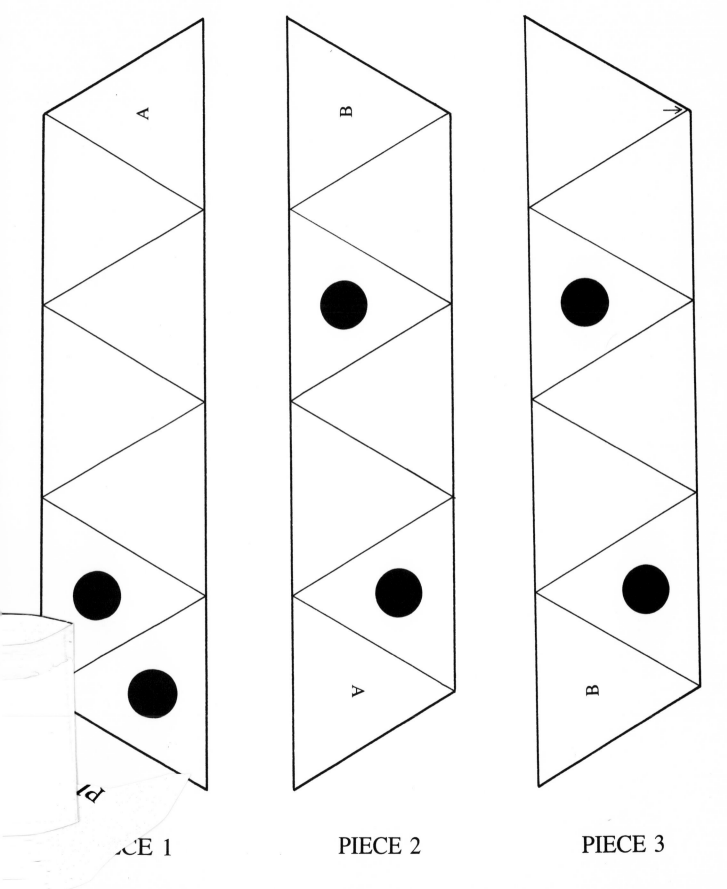

PIECE 1   PIECE 2   PIECE 3

THE THREE RINGS

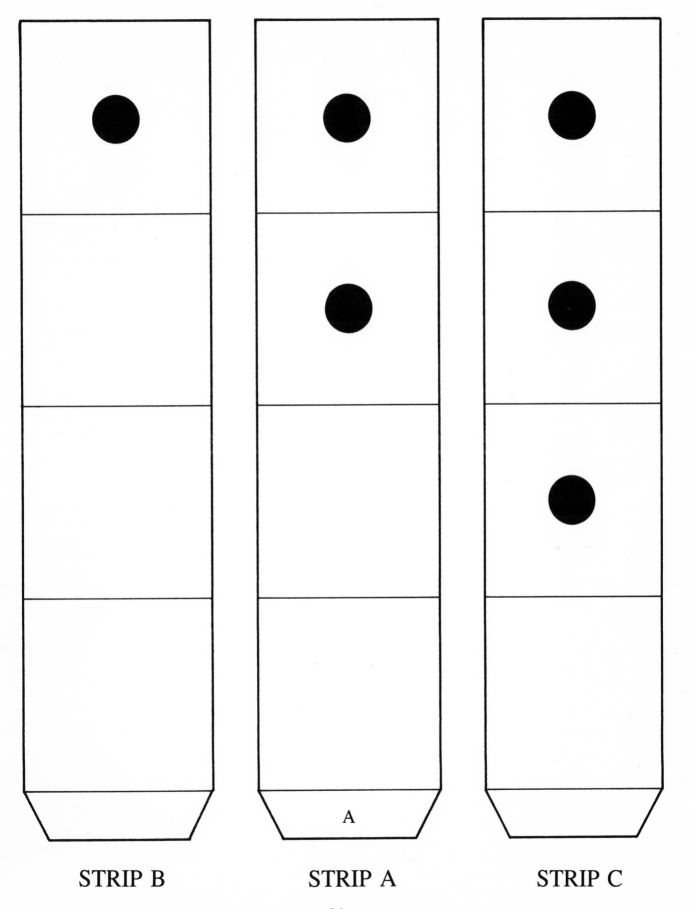

STRIP B   STRIP A   STRIP C

THE LINKED RINGS

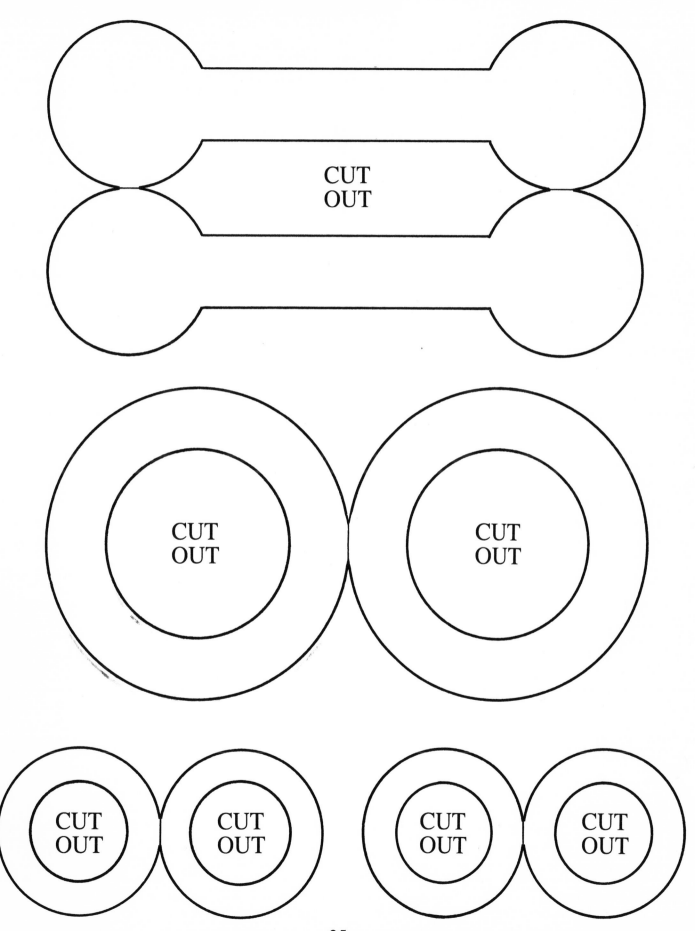

THE FOLDING STAR

THE SLIDING BLOCKS

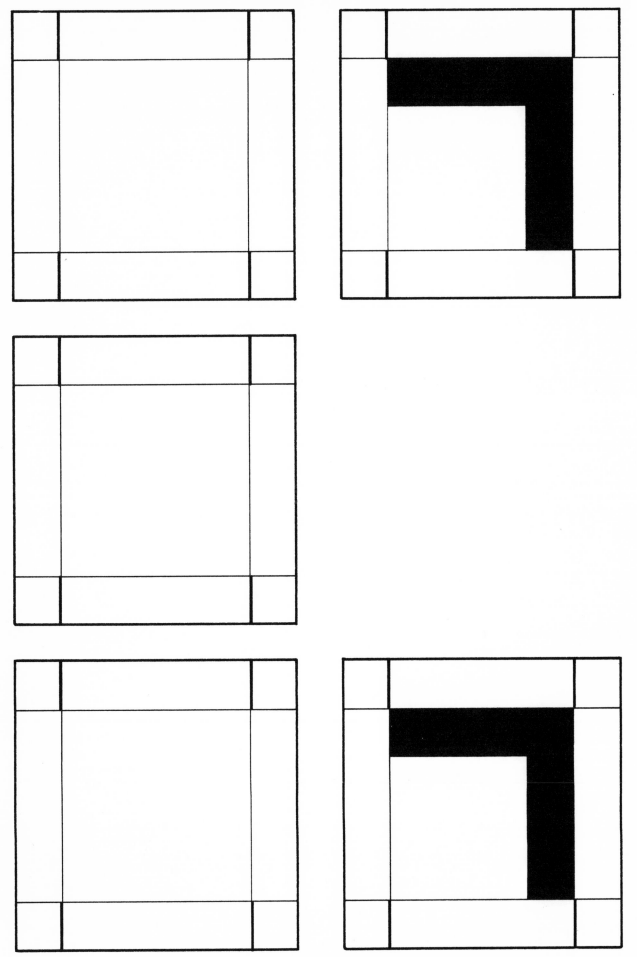

THE TESSERA

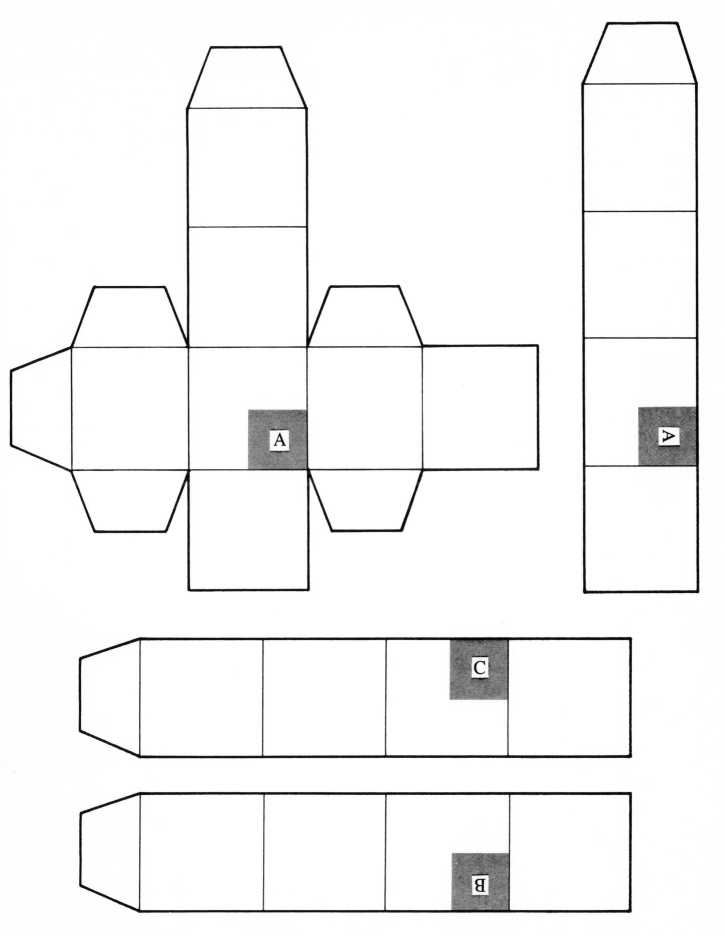

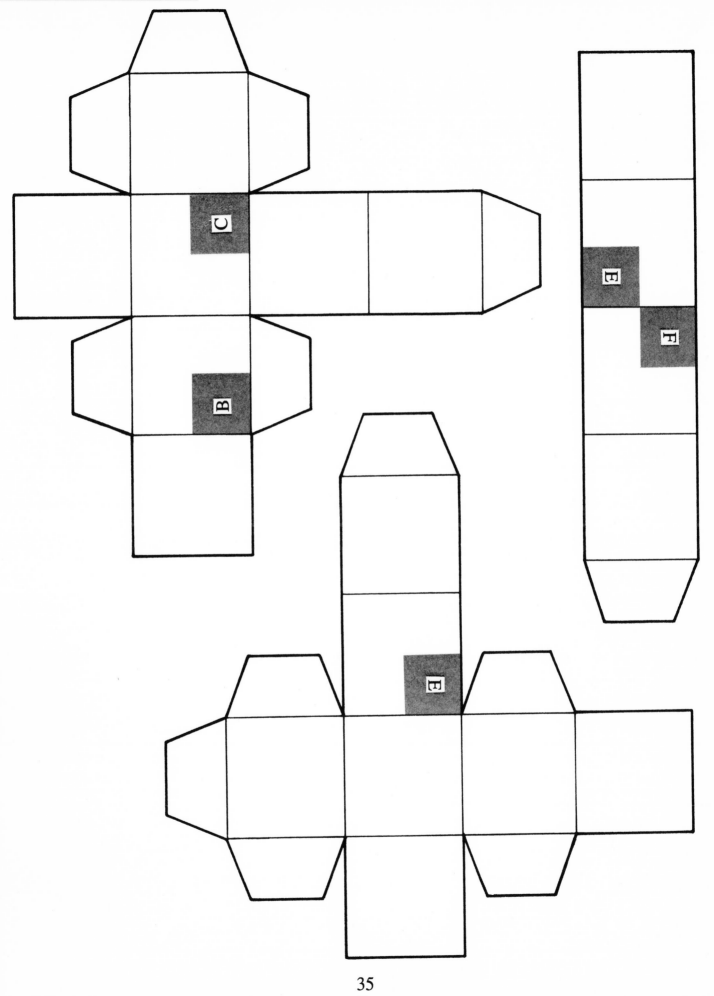

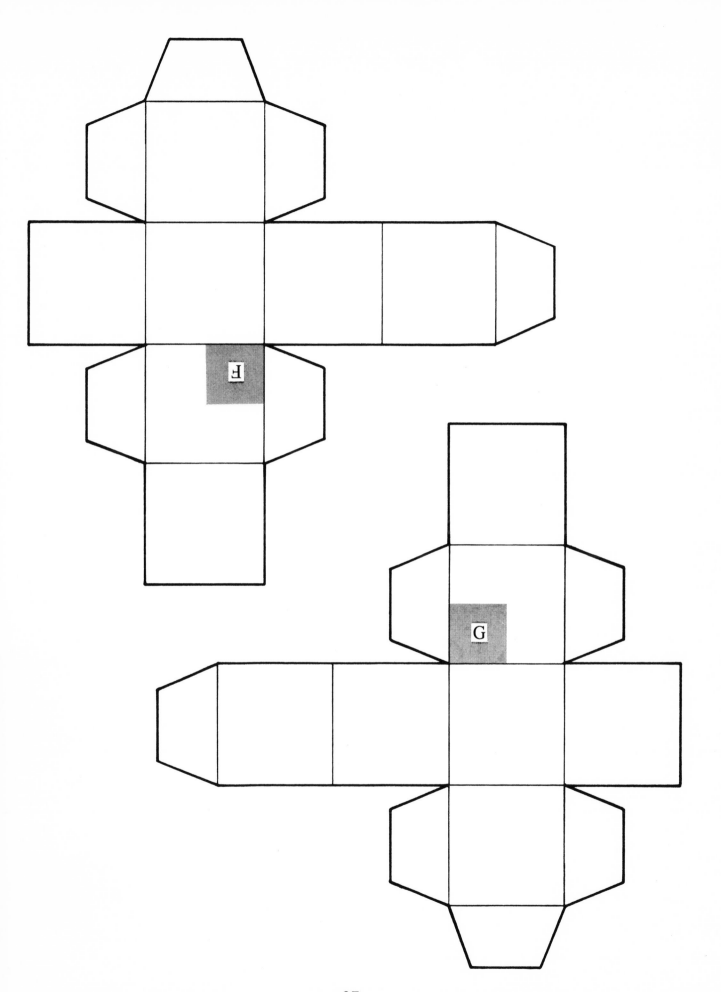

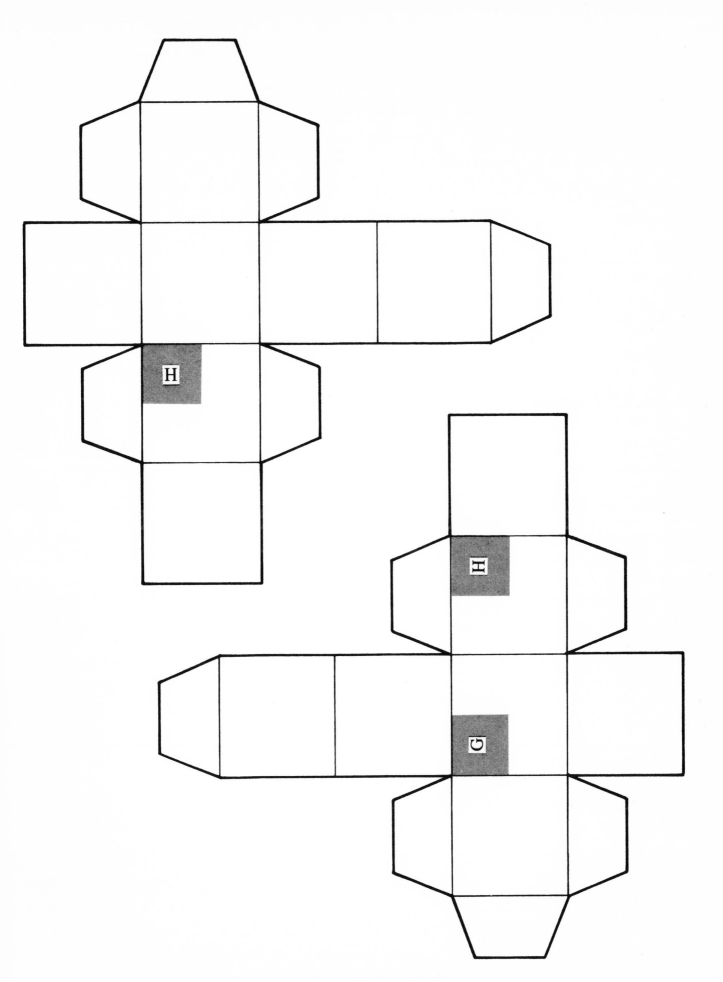

THE WALKING MAZE

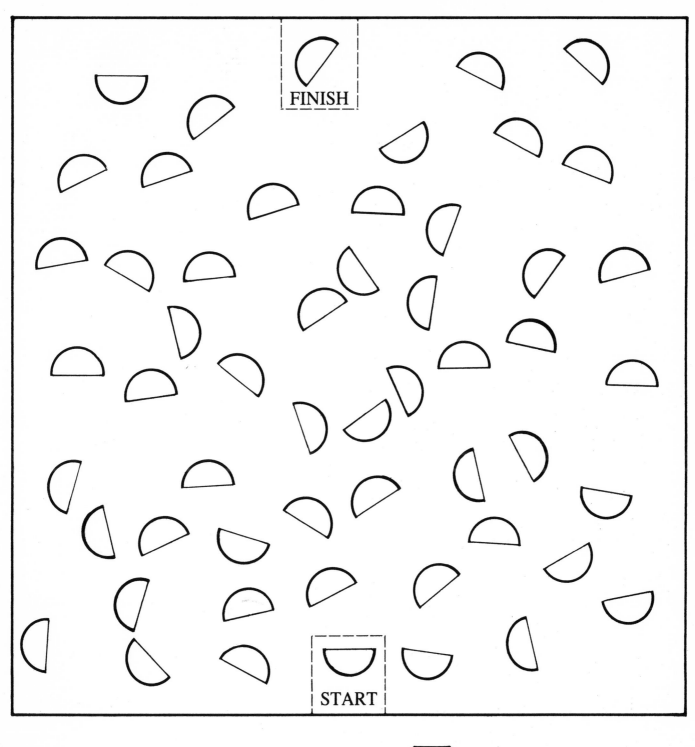

FINISH

START

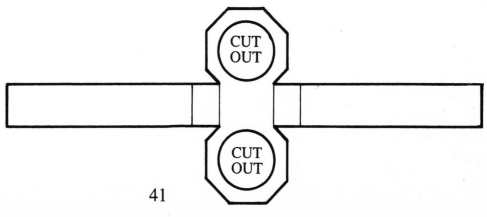

CUT
OUT

CUT
OUT

41

THE REVERSING CUBE

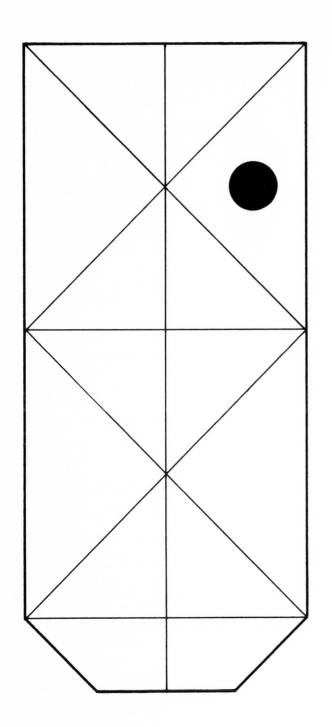
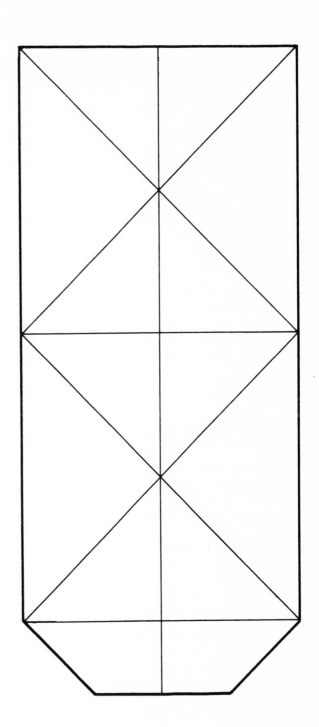

SOLUTIONS

THE MAGIC PYRAMID

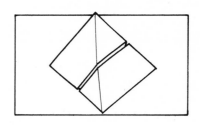

The solution to this one is simple. Just match up the two square sides face to face and turn one of the pieces until the pyramid is formed as shown.

THE FOUR CUBES

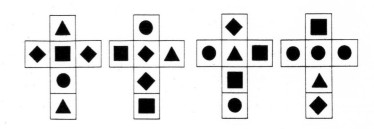

Here is the pattern for the solution. Find the cube with the matching arrangement for each position and turn it accordingly.

THE FLEXAGON

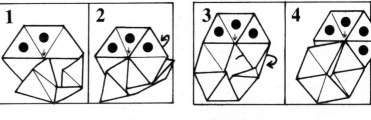

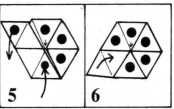

1. Find the triangle with the small arrow and dot and hold it in an inverted position as shown in Figure 1. We'll refer to this as triangle #1.

2. The triangle attached directly to it on the left has a dot. The one attached directly on the right does not. We'll call both of these triangles #2. The rest of the triangles, on each side of the chain, will continue to be numbered in this manner.

3. Fold triangle #3 on the left down and back behind triangle #2 on the left. Then fold triangle #3 on the right down and forward, covering triangle #2 on the right. This will reveal a third dot (Figure 2).

4. Fold triangle #5 on the right to the back, then bring triangles #6 and #7 together around and forward to put the fourth dot in place (Figures 3–4).

5. The fifth dot is now hidden on the lowest inverted triangle. Fold that triangle up into position, while lifting the triangles connected to it (Figure 5).

6. Finally fold the triangle containing the last dot down and away so that it is facing the back of the hexagon. Then fold this outer triangle back up into the hexagon to complete the puzzle (Figure 6).

THE THREE RINGS

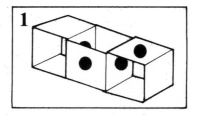

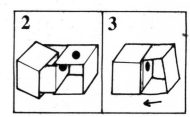

1. Hold the rings in a line as shown (Figure 1). Note that the single dot on the left ring faces inside the middle ring, while the middle dot on the right ring faces inside the middle ring.

2. Pivot the left ring into the middle one so that it forms a cube (Figure 2).

3. Now slip the upper and lower sides of the right ring inside the upper and lower sides of the left ring and push the right ring into the assembly to form the cube with no dots showing (Figure 3).

45

SOLUTIONS

THE LINKED RINGS

We'll show you the procedure for unlinking the rings. To link them, just reverse the steps.

1. Start by bending the large middle ring toward you just enough to slip the small ring on the right over it and onto the left ring, but not enough to crease the large ring (Figure 1).

2. Now slide all three rings over to the right as far as possible and push the right barbell back through the opening in the large ring (Figure 2).

3. Now slide all the rings over to the left, bend the large ring again (but not enough to crease it), and slide both smaller rings over it and off (Figure 3).

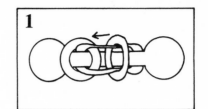
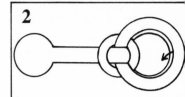
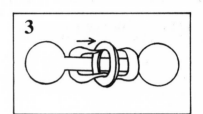

THE FOLDING STAR

1. Hold the star with the inner cut at the lower left as indicated (Figure 1). The body of the elephant we will use appears on the bottom triangle.

2. Bring the topmost triangle containing the tail down and around in back and up into a position to the left of the body. This puts the tail in place (Figure 2).

3. Now fold the triangle with the tail back to form the left side of a three-sided pyramid, with the body in front (Figure 3).

4. You now have a pyramid with a flap coming off the back edge. Fold that flap in half, then in half again (Figure 4). This will reveal a head part that can be folded onto the third side of the pyramid to complete the body. This three-dimensional view of the elephant around the sides of a pyramid is the only way to solve the puzzle. The elephant cannot be formed if the triangles are flat.

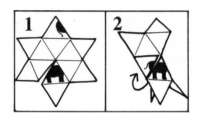
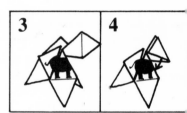

THE SLIDING BLOCKS

Start with the blocks in the beginning position and imagine that the spaces in the tray are numbered as shown. The sequence below shows the correct moves to make; the numbers indicate the block that must be moved by its position on the tray.

3-6-5-2-1-4-5-6-3-2-5-4-1-2-3-6-5

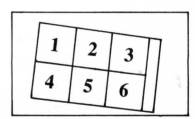

SOLUTIONS

THE TESSERA

1. Take the piece made up of three cubes and hold it as shown in Figure 1.

2. Now take the piece with two cubes and one ring, hold it as shown, and slip the ring over the right-hand cube on the first piece (Figure 2).

3. Hold the piece made of one cube and one ring as shown, and slip the ring over the leftmost cube of the assembly (Figure 3).

4. Finally hold the last piece, made of one cube and two rings, above the assembly as shown, then slip both rings over the topmost cubes of the assembly (Figure 4).

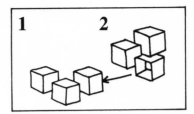
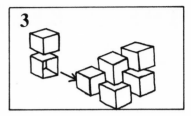

THE WALKING MAZE

The illustration at the right shows the correct sequence of moves.

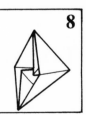

THE REVERSING CUBE

This one's a little tricky, so follow the steps carefully.

1. Press down on opposite sides to flatten the strip into a square (Figure 1).

2. Fold corners A and B down and together to create a triangle (Figure 2).

3. Push the opposite corners C and D together and the inner flaps in opposite directions, to form another smaller square (Figure 3).

4. Pull out on point E (Figure 3) and press the flap down flat. Do the same on the back side to create a rectangle (Figures 4–5).

5. Squeeze in on opposite sides F and G to create another rectangle (Figure 6).

6. Now reverse steps 1 to 5 by pulling down on flap H and similarly on the back to return to the square (Figure 7). Then open up the square back into the triangle (Figure 8) and open further into the ring. The reverse side should now be on the outside of the ring.

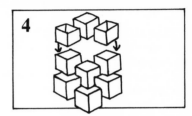
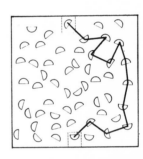
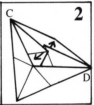
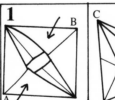
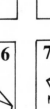
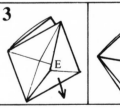
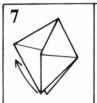

47